Henry David Thoreau, Sophia E. Thoreau, Samuel Arthur Jones

Some Unpublished Letters of Henry D. and Sophia E. Thoreau

A Chapter in the History of a Still-Born Book

Henry David Thoreau, Sophia E. Thoreau, Samuel Arthur Jones

Some Unpublished Letters of Henry D. and Sophia E. Thoreau
A Chapter in the History of a Still-Born Book

ISBN/EAN: 9783744711708

Printed in Europe, USA, Canada, Australia, Japan

Cover: Foto ©ninafisch / pixelio.de

More available books at **www.hansebooks.com**

Henry D. Thoreau, age 44.
From an ambrotype by Dunshee, of New Bedford, Mass., taken in August, 1861. Thoreau died the following spring.

SOME UNPUBLISHED LETTERS OF HENRY D. AND SOPHIA E. THOREAU

A CHAPTER IN THE HISTORY OF A STILL-BORN BOOK

"He noblest lives and noblest dies who makes and keeps his self-made laws."
    The Kasidah of Hájí Abdú El-Yezdi.

EDITED WITH A PREFATORY NOTE
BY
SAMUEL ARTHUR JONES

PRINTED ON THE MARION PRESS
JAMAICA, QUEENSBOROUGH, NEW-YORK
1899

Copyright, 1898, by
SAMUEL ARTHUR JONES.

ILLUSTRATIONS.

OPP. PAGE

Henry D. Thoreau, age 44 . Title
Home of the Thoreau family . 22
Henry D. Thoreau, age 39 . . 37
Henry D. Thoreau, age 37 . . 53
Sophia E. Thoreau 72
Burial-plot of the Thoreau family 80

From negatives by
ALFRED W. HOSMER,
Concord, Mass.

PREFATORY NOTE.

LEARNING that Thoreau had once a Western correspondent, and knowing that these of his letters had not been published, it occurred to the slightly irascible and somewhat eccentric ex-professor that it were worth while to make search therefor: possibly that correspondence might be recovered. Thoreau's correspondent was found without difficulty,—an aged and venerable man,—and to the great surprise of the ex-professor the holographs were transferred to his keeping, and are used by the present editor in preparing the text of this book.

Thoreau's letters are in themselves but a trifle, yet they give characteristic glimpses of him; those of his sister reveal a phase of his character that is not so widely known as it deserves, and in justice to a dead man should be.

The story of these simple letters is briefly as follows: George Ripley's review of *Walden; or, Life in the Woods,* led a distant reader to write to Ticknor and Company for a copy, the chief incitement being the liberal citations from the book itself. Upon receiving the volume it was almost literally devoured; a somewhat peculiar spiritual experience had prepared the way for it with that remote reader; he then found it sweet in the mouth, and after forty years it has not proven bitter in the belly.

Of course the book had "found" its reader, as Coleridge would say of such a divine conjunction, and like the famishing charity boy, that particular reader wanted "some more." That earnest man, reading *Walden*, and one of the few of that day able to read it 'between the lines,'—reading and pondering under the burr-oaks in the silence of the forest solitude,—

"—felt like some watcher of the skies
When a new planet swims into his
  ken."

From the title-page of *Walden* he learned that Thoreau was also the author of another book, *A Week on the Concord and Merrimack Rivers*. Failing to obtain a copy of this from the publishers of *Walden* or any other source then known to him, the seeker managed to get Thoreau's address and made application directly to him; and there the correspondence begins.

Thoreau and his Western correspondent never met, though at one point of the hopeless journey to Minnesota in search of health one hour's ride would have brought them together; but the doomed pilgrim knew that he must speedily return to put his house in order, for he was not deceived in regard to his bodily condition. "I think," he wrote to Mr. Ricketson, "that, on the whole, my health is better than when you were here; but my faith in the doctors has not increased."

The correspondence with Sophia E. Thoreau arose from a letter of condolence, on the death of her brother, written more than a month after that event. A subsequent visit to Concord brought the distant friend and the Thoreau survivors face to face: it was the *res angustæ domi* alone that had prevented such a meeting with Thoreau himself. The visitor from afar was tenderly received by both the mourning mother and sister and Thoreau's friends Alcott and Channing. Before returning, the pilgrim was requested by both Mrs. Thoreau and Sophia to select from the library of his departed friend some books for keepsakes. Thus it came that both the ex-professor and the present editor saw and touched the very copy of Lemprière's *Classical Dictionary* that had been Thoreau's when he was an undergraduate in Harvard College,—the first flyleaf bearing the autograph: "D. H. Thoreau." This is written in ink, while on the succeeding leaf is the pencilled inscription, "Mr. . . . from S. E. Thoreau." The book selected as a memento for the visitor's wife is an American edition of *The Spectator*, two volumes in one, Philadelphia, 1832. On the title-page is an autograph, in a fine clerkly hand: "J. Thoreau." It is the signature of Thoreau's father, a man, according to one biographer, "who led a plodding, unambitious and respectable life in Concord village." It is not mentioned whether he 'kept a gig'; but commend us always to the 'plodder' who, from his scanty means, provides his family book-shelf with a substantially bound and well printed copy of the *Spectator*. One can readily believe that such a man was respected, gigless though he be; but few would have the hardihood to declare that a father who furnishes the *Spectator* for his children's reading is 'unambitious.' Perhaps the highest ambition lies in a wise forecast that is not for one's self;

"But Brutus says he was (un)ambitious;
 And Brutus is an *honorable* man."

The sterling native worth of Thoreau's Western correspondent was quickly discerned by not only Thoreau's mother and sister: Thoreau's friends recognized and honored it. The transparent-souled Alcott was moved to the highest issues of friendship, as sundry inscribed presentation copies of the writings of that belated Platonist amply testify; and William Ellery Channing, the "man of genius, and of the moods that sometimes make genius an unhappy boon," was thawed into human warmth, as specially inscribed copies of his books — perhaps the most elusive "first (and only that) editions" that ever mocked the book-hunter's desire — amply show, on those precious shelves, where the ex-professor and the present editor saw them for the first and only time. One who has been allowed access to those richly laden shelves may be allowed, without violating the sanctity of hospitality, to bear witness to the simplicity, sincerity, and serenity investing the eventide of a true life with that ineffable splendor which has in it the soul's strongest assurance of a dayspring beyond the mists of Life's mirage.

The Froude letter and that which authenticates it are not considered irrelevant. The English historian's letter to the Concord "loafer" is introduced to show that although his first book was 'despised and rejected' of men, Thoreau had the assurances that are always vouchsafed to the solitary thinker, and these from sources so diverse as Oxford University, justly proud of the achievements of its scholars, and the primeval oak forest of a remote young State,—a raw settlement, as it had been called only fifty years before.* It is not whence the apprehension, the agreement, the assent; it is who agrees, assents, and by the cordial handgrasp conveys

---

* "At Ypsilanti I picked up an Ann Arbor newspaper. It was badly printed, but its contents were good; and it could happen nowhere out of America that so raw a settlement as that at Ann Arbor, where there is difficulty in procuring decent accommodations, should have a newspaper."

Harriet Martineau. *Society in America.*

to the solitary scholar, whose meditations have disturbed Mammon's market-place, the calm, unfaltering courage that is ever a marvel to the multitude, which quietly 'bears the fardels' of unthinking servitude.

The difference between the fibre of a Froude and a Thoreau will be quickly distinguished by those who have read the exculpatory preface especially written for the second edition of Froude's *Nemesis of Faith*. Froude faced the angry storm of incensed detraction with the courage of a well-equipped scholar and the dignity of a true gentleman; nevertheless he had made an 'explanation': not the whole world could have moved Thoreau's lips to anything other than a smile of infinite commiseration; he would not have foregone a single furlong of his accustomed 'walk'; he might indeed have whispered to his own heart,

"Time cannot bend the line which
Truth hath writ."

The present editor has assured himself that Froude's presentation copy of his self-sacrificing *Nemesis of Faith* is to this day in Emerson's library at the old home, but he has not been able to learn that Froude also sent a copy to Thoreau; so it is a safe inference that Thoreau read Emerson's. A phrase in Froude's letter to Thoreau shows conclusively that Thoreau had learned of Froude from Emerson and that Thoreau had read Froude's ill-starred *Nemesis* — the "wild protest against all authority, Divine and human," as that gentlest of Quakeresses, Caroline Fox, terms it. Froude writes this phrase within inverted commas: "not on account of his [Emerson's] word, but because I myself have read and know you." This can refer only to a complimentary copy of *A Week on the Concord and Merrimack Rivers* that had been previously sent to Froude either by Thoreau or their mutual friend Emerson. Thoreau himself has recorded that of his still-born book some 'seventy-five copies were given away.'

Froude's *Nemesis of Faith* could transmit no seismic tremors to the man who would have nothing between him and Heaven—not even a rafter. The blue dome with its inscrutable mystery: nothing must obstruct the soul's view of that! The chapter in Thoreau's *Week* entitled "Sunday" could readily carry to Froude the assurance that possibly he, too, had

"Builded better than he knew,"

that very possibly the angry Anglican hierarchy had merely mistaken a Church colic for a universal cataclysm.

These two recalcitrants never touched hands, albeit the 'steam bridges' were both commodious and convenient. Their perigeum occurred during Froude's much later visit to Emerson, and it was in Sleepy Hollow burying-ground; but that perihelion was sadly incomplete: six feet of graveyard mould and death, the mystery of mysteries, intervened. For both of them *now*, no more of that mystery. Oh, the boon of 'crossing the bar'!

A word in regard to the unusual manner in which the Letters are presented to the reader. One with whom, of all men living, the present editor is best acquainted (an effete ex-professor, gouty, grouty, and gray-headed) made these Letters the subject of a lecture delivered in aid of a Women's Gymnasium ("More power to their elbows!" said the ex-professor) located—it is not necessary to specify where. The text as written for that occasion has been followed: a convenience which all editors will fully appreciate. At the risk of marring the symmetry of the printed page the labor-saving editor will take the liberty of superposing such patches of his own plain homespun upon the ex-professor's tapestry as occasion seems to demand (though he may be tempted of the devil to take undue advantage of so rare an opportunity). Being himself "as mild a mannered man as ever cut a throat," he owes it to himself to gently but plainly deprecate the ex-professor's lapses into the sarcastic. Both the editor and Herr Teufelsdröckh believe that sarcasm is the Devil's patois. As that is perilous stuff, he'll have none of it; the ex-professor must stand for his own petard: a proposition which he will be the last man to reject.

The typewritten text of the ex-professor's lecture is disfigured with pen-and-ink interlineations, and this is something so unusual that one who knows him so well as doth the editor could not resist the very natural curiosity which led to the asking for an explanation. This, as it fell from the ex-professor's lips, is too characteristic of him to be withheld; so it shall be shared with the reader—though this complaisance involves the editor in not a little personal peril.

Be it known then, first of all, that the ex-professor himself takes Thoreau very seriously; does not by any possible interpretation consider *him* a "glittering generality," but rather a "blazing ubiquity" wherever and whenever the blunt, plain truth is needful—which time and place he also believes is always and everywhere. Perhaps an excerpt from the ex-professor's lecture on "Thoreau" will best serve to show his attitude. (This lecture, it may be as well to add, was written for and delivered in a nameless territory where 'success' is a matter of the bank-book rather than of that old-fashioned Hebrew Book.)

"I am chiefly desirous of enforcing one consideration regarding this man Thoreau, namely: that the brief episode in his life by which he is commonly known—the shanty life at Walden Pond—was not the vagary of an enthusiast. Reared in a family to every member of which 'life was something more than a parade of pretensions, a conflict of ambition or an incessant scramble for the common objects of desire,' Thoreau never lost sight of the high ideal which inspired that humble household.

"While yet an undergraduate he believed that the mere beauty of this world transcended far all the convenience to which luxury would debase it. He then thought 'the order of things should be somewhat reversed; the seventh should be man's day of toil, wherein to earn his living by the sweat of his brow, and the other six his Sabbath of the affections and the soul,—in which to range this widespread garden, and drink in the soft influences and sublime revelations of Nature.'

"With darkened eyes Milton dreamed of Paradise Lost; with an unfaltering trust in the beneficence of God Thoreau went forth in the broad daylight to find it. Who shall say of him that he failed of his quest; who shall declare to the struggling millions of Earth's toilers that Paradise is, indeed, irretrievably lost!

"Once before there came to the race a man wearing a garment of camel's hair, eating locusts and wild honey, and bearing a Message: perhaps this, too, is the veiled purpose of him who abode in that much-derided shanty at Walden Pond.

"Do we not hear the sounds as of satanic revelry coming from high places in the land; is not every breeze burdened with the muttered curses of ill-requited labor toiling for the task-masters until the sweat of the brow is that of a Gethsemane which is only the Devil's?

"The message-bringer to the nineteenth century said: *Simplify your lives!* It is indeed a simple message, but it is fraught with terrible meaning for us all. If the foundations of this republic are to remain unshaken in the stress of the struggle that is even now looming darkly before us, it is the application, by *all*, of Thoreau's teachings that will avert or mitigate the disaster; if the end is to be only ravined ruin, then will his memory live in Literature as our everlasting reproach."

Verily our ex-professor doth take Thoreau seriously; but there are other matters that he takes as seriously, namely, the *misconceptions* of Thoreau by all and sundry ineptitudes; and on such occasions the ex-professor certainly forgets the amenities — but righteous wrath hath also its own peculiar *Amen!* Having said this much, it is due the reader that he should be allowed to get a glimpse of the ex-professor in a 'spate.' Here is an instance from the same lecture:

"Now let us return to the shanty at Walden Pond wherein Thoreau dwelt alone for some two and a half years, supporting himself solely by his own labor and living so 'close to the bone.' Lowell has written that Thoreau went there in the self-assertive mood of a hermit whose seclusion is a declaration of his non-dependence upon civilization. 'His shanty life was a mere impossibility, so far as his own conception of it goes, as an entire independency of mankind. The tub of Diogenes has a sounder bottom. Thoreau's experiment actually presupposed all that complicated civilization which it theoretically abjured. He squatted upon another man's land; he borrows an axe; his boards, his nails, his bricks, his mortar, his books, his lamp, his fish-hooks, his plough, his hoe, all turn state's evidence against him as an accomplice in the sin of that artificial civilization which rendered it possible that such a person as Henry D. Thoreau should exist at all.' I question whether in all the history of criticism a blinder misconception can be found."

[Just here the ex-professor was

evidently heated. He took the customary sip of water with which the professional lecturer prepares his learned larynx for its next innings. Having returned the handkerchief to the left hand coat-tail pocket, the ex-professor resumed.]

"In the two royal-octavo volumes edited by Professor Norton, *Letters of James Russell Lowell,* there is a photogravure showing the poet sitting on the ground, by the bole of an ancient elm. His hat is off, his hair is parted in the middle (and this was fifty years ago!), his head is thrown forward so as to put his face in the most favorable position for pictorial effect; his whole attitude is of studied ease, and the hand nearest the spectator is—kid-gloved! Oh, the significance of that picture! Posing under an elm in whose branches the robins had built their nests long before the Norsemen's prow had grated upon the sands of the New England coast; the small birds singing around the petted poet, the fragrance of summer filling the air, the scented breeze toying with his curled locks, and he carrying into *that* sanctuary—the kid glove of 'Society'! Is this the man to comprehend the aim and purpose of Thoreau,—this leather and prunella combination of 'civilization' and 'culture'!

"Yes; I am aware that I am speaking of a dead man, of a man whose pig weighed more than he thought it would, if one may judge from the tone of his own early letters; of one whose living tongue tasted the seducing sweetness of earthly fame; but there is another dead man, one who was called away 'in the midst of his broken task, which none else can finish,' and him the kid-gloved favorite of fame and fashion has flouted. There is a time for all things; a time for the sweet charity of silence, a time also for asserting the grandeur of simple and sincere manhood: brown-handed manhood that never saluted Nature with a kid glove. *De mortuis nil nisi bonum?* Yes; I'll stand by that sentiment; but it can also be read, *De mortuis nil nisi verum:* it is well also to stand by that!

"It was Thoreau's purpose at Walden Pond to find out just how much of Lowell's confessedly 'complicated civilization' was absolutely necessary in order that Man's sojourn in Nature might be as sane and serene as became an immortal soul. Did he not plainly write, 'I went to the woods because I wished to live deliberately, to front only the essential facts of life [kid gloves not being found in that inventory], and see if I could not learn what it had to teach, and not, when I came to die, discover that I had not lived. I did not wish to live what was not life, living is so dear; nor did I wish to practice resignation, unless it was quite necessary. I wanted to live deep and suck all the marrow out of life, to live so sturdily and Spartan-like as to put to rout all that was not life, to cut a broad swath and shave close, to drive life into a corner, and reduce it to its lowest terms, and, if it proved to be mean, why then to get the whole and genuine meanness of it, and publish its meanness to the world; or if it were sublime, to know it by experience, and be able to give a true account of it in my next excursion.'

"*In my next excursion*—that journey made with closed eyes and folded hands; hands not kid-gloved; bare hands to lay hold on the realities beyond this Vanity Fair that we in our ignorance call 'Life.'

"Of a truth, Lowell, a clergyman's son, could not read the simple chart by which the son of the Concord pencil-maker shaped his course amidst the sunken rocks of Conventionality."

But the ex-professor's foibles are making us forget the pen-and-ink interlineations that are yet awaiting their explanations.

"I did not imagine," said the ex-professor on the morning after his lecture on the Letters, "that any but sensible people would sit an hour to hear an old fellow talk about Thoreau; but, sir, on going to the appointed place, I found myself, and most unexpectedly, facing a parlour full of frills and fine linen. An exceedingly well-dressed young man sat down at the piano, and he was immediately joined by another even more extraordinarily arrayed. One played and the other warbled something in a tongue unknown to the builders of Babel, I'll warrant. I have never in all my life felt so much out of place since the only woman to whom I ever proposed laughed outright in my face. But there was no escape; I was fairly in for it, and I did some curious thinking whilst that nice young man was warbling. The music ceased, and there was a small storm of kid-gloved handclapping. That disconcerted me still more; for there was my audience applauding some artistic noise which I felt in my very bones they did not understand. I had to make peace with myself before I could begin with my exposition of the Thoreau letters; so I just told them right out what I had been thinking of whilst they were listening to that incomprehensible singing. I told them I had been thinking of the rude homeliness of that shanty at Walden Pond, and that my peculiar environment just then nearly paralyzed me, and only that I had the courage of my convictions, I could not read the Thoreau letters then and there. Just then a distinguished-looking gentleman, with the greatest expanse of shirt-front I had ever seen during all my earthly career, adjusted an English monocle to his right eye and politely stared at me. Worse than all, it had not entered my mind that I should have bought a pair of kid gloves for the occasion.

"It is astonishing how much 'punishment' well-bred people will take fully as smilingly as do all the 'fancy'; but I held them down, sir, for a full hour of torment; and certainly some things got into the talk that were not in the text. The next day a friend, whose wife was present, told me that when she was putting on her cloak, behind a screen in the robing room, she heard one ultra-fashionable lady say to another of the same species: "Well, I never was *bored* so in all my life!" Then I knew that I had scored a success.—Suppose I had talked down to the level of her comprehension!"

The ex-professor thereupon filled his pipe; the present editor found himself filled with reflections of which there is no need to make farther mention.

SOME UNPUBLISHED LETTERS OF HENRY D. AND SOPHIA E. THOREAU.

SOME UNPUBLISHED LETTERS OF HENRY D. AND SOPHIA E. THOREAU.

I.

THE FROUDE EPISODE.

How strangely human lives are interlinked: the chain of influences beginning and ending how little we know where and when. At the first reading of Emerson's *Each and All,* who is not startled by the lines—

Nor knowest thou what argument
Thy life to thy neighbor's creed hath lent.

Is not that enquiry a 'flash-light' for the soul?

Into these mysterious relations and influences Time and Space enter not. Far remote is the little monastery at Zwolle, and five centuries have passed since the meekest of pietists put aside his pen, but if there is in this world to-day a spiritual influence of potent puissance it is Thomas of Kempen's *Imitatio Christi*. The serene monk has vanished, and only Omniscience knoweth what argument his secluded life hath lent to the variant creeds of millions, who are now his 'neighbors' in that *Civitas Dei* the son of Monica has made known to us.

Say you, All that was so long ago! Well, would it lose anything of its mysteriousness if it were of this downright to-day? That which we call "to-day" also hath its mysteries, and not the least of them is this interlinking of our lives through and by these occult influences.

Here we are gathered to-night, some five hundred and twenty years after the birth of Thomas à Kempis, avowing his influence upon our lives. He that was Thomas à Kempis had lain in his grave twenty-one years before the prow of the *Pinta* was pointed towards the New World, yet here are we upon a beautiful peninsula—"*Peninsulam amœnam*"—therein, and actually indebted to a lady now in Italy, and whom it is little likely that any one of us hath ever met,—indebted, I say, to this remote stranger for the privilege of reading a letter written fifty years ago, never yet published, and having an interesting bearing upon the matter that you have come together to hear about.

"145 Via Rasella, Rome,
Dec'r 17, 1897.

"Really, there is not much to tell about the Froude letter. Miss Sophia Thoreau sent for me, a few weeks before her death, to give me some last instructions and to ask my assistance in distributing personal things; and at the same time she gave me several letters for myself, among them this, knowing that I would value them as autographs.

"My impression is that she feared people would think it too flattering, and for that or some other reason she did not at that time care to have it published.

"She gave me other letters and manuscripts, requesting me to place them with my own hands in one of the trunks deposited in the Concord

Town Library, which were to be passed on to Mr. Blake (I think that was his name); I mean Thoreau's literary executor. Had she wished this letter to be published she would undoubtedly have placed it with the manuscripts which I was to put in one of the boxes from which Mr. Blake was to select material for publication.

"I once showed it to Mr. Emerson, who thought Mr. Blake should see it at once; but as it was given to me and not to him, and as I felt certain Miss Thoreau did not wish it published at that time, I did not act upon this advice.

"I have often wondered why she did not put it with the papers which were to be placed in the box of manuscripts. Her action was no doubt intentional, as we read the letter over together about three weeks before her death: at the same time, I think there can be no harm in publishing it now."

So far as pertains to our purpose to-night I might go on at once to the Froude letter, but in so doing I should shirk a duty to the dead, for the discharging of which I am sure you will allow me a few moments.

If you should open a certain Life of Thoreau you could read therein, "Mrs. Thoreau, with her sister Louisa, and her sisters-in-law, Sarah, Maria, and Jane Thoreau, took their share in the village bickerings"; and also that Mrs. Thoreau indulged in "sharp and sudden flashes of gossip and malice": this and much else that is derogatory. Now Mrs. Thoreau died in 1873, and yet, in 1897, and so casually, the lady whose letter I am reading thus testifies to the high quality of the women of the Thoreau family:

"The women of the Thoreau family seem to me quite as remarkable as the men; and people who knew John Thoreau considered him even cleverer and more promising than Henry and greatly lamented his untimely death. Certainly both Helen, whom I never knew, and Sophia, whom I knew well, were exceptionally clever women. Sophia was extremely witty, a brilliant conversationalist, and her love of nature made her the most delightful of companions for a ramble through the woods and meadows.

"'Aunt Maria' was, at the time I knew her, a sweet, gentle old lady who occasionally wrote me charming letters. Mrs. Thoreau, Henry's mother, was full of kind feeling for everybody, and had a generous, helpful spirit. She was most kind to all the children of her acquaintance, often devising entertainments for them; and I still have a vivid recollection of the boxes of home-made sweets she used to send to me when I was away at school."

Are you quite ready to believe that "gossip and malice" could find an abiding place in such a heart as this?

Now have we reached the letter written when Froude had burned his ships and was submitted to the slings and arrows of the "black dragoons" on whom John Sterling had also turned his back.

Manchester, September 3, 1849.
Dear Mr. Thoreau:

I have long intended to write to you, to thank you for that noble expression of yourself you were good enough to send me. I know not why I have not done so; except from a foolish sense that I should not write until I had thought of something to say that it would be worth your while to read.

What can I say to you except express the honour and the love I feel for you. An honour and a love which Emerson taught me long ago to feel, but which I feel now 'not on account of his word, but because I myself have read and know you.'

When I think of what you are— of what you have done as well as what you have written, I have the right to tell you that there is no man living upon this earth at present, whose friendship or whose notice I value more than yours.

What are these words! yet I wished to say something—and I must use words, though they serve but seldom in these days for much but lies.

In your book and in one other from your side of the Atlantic, "Margaret," I see hope for the coming world; all else which I have found true in any of our thinkers (or even yours) is their flat denial of what is false in the modern popular jargon—but for their positive affirming side, they do but fling us back upon our own human nature to hold on by that with our own strength. A few men *here and there do this as the later Romans did—but* mankind *cannot, and I have gone near to despair. I am growing not to despair, and I thank you for a helping hand.*

Well, I must see you some time or other. It is not such a great matter with these steam bridges. I wish to shake hands with you and look a brave man in the face. In the meantime I will but congratulate you on the age in which your work is cast: the world has never seen one more pregnant.

God bless you!

Your friend (if you will let him call you so),

J. A. Froude.

There is so much between the lines here that one must go back to the middle of the present century for a clue. In 1849 Froude, then a Fellow of Exeter College, Oxford, published a book — *The Nemesis of Faith* — which, immediately following in the wake of the "Oxford Movement," gave a disagreeable shock to Anglican Churchmen, lay and cleric. The scholarly Fellow of Exeter College had been coquetting with Catholicism. He had managed to lose the faith of his fathers, but had utterly failed to find any surrogate; before him surged a weltering waste, pitiless storm, and blinding darkness, and no place whereon to plant his way-worn feet.

The obnoxious book was burned in the quadrangle by the Senior Fellow of Oriel College; "the old, familiar faces" either looked askance at the audacious doubter or were wholly averted; the Quarterlies were flooded with condemnatory reviews, in which even lay journalism participated,— and this in America as well as Great

Britain,—and the author's every hope of place and preferment in the Established Church perished beyond all expectation of resurrection: for him there was no "benefit of the clergy." It was a pitiful immolation, because a self-immolation. As Carlyle grimly told Froude—he should have "burned his own smoke."

The Nemesis of Faith is not a wholesome book to read, because it is not the doubt that is born of mental and therefore spiritual health. One need only read Froude's previous publication, *The Shadows of the Clouds,* to discover the morbid mind. *The Nemesis of Faith* is wholly destructive—and in such high matters it is so fatally easy to destroy—it has not the shadow of an endeavor to provide a shelter for the soul: *that* is left naked, houseless, and homeless to the pitiless peltings of the storm of doubt and unbelief. It was a moral suicide in a moment of desperate aberration,—a soul's tragedy.

Emerson knew some time before that something of this nature was imminent. He wrote in his journal for April, 1848: "I had an old invitation from Mr. Clough, a Fellow of Oriel, and last week I had a new one from Dr. Daubeny, the botanical professor. I went on Thursday. I was housed close upon Oriel, though not within it, but I lived altogether upon college hospitalities, dining at Exeter College with Palgrave, Froude, and other Fellows, and breakfasting next morning at Oriel with Clough, Dr. Daubeny, etc. They all showed me the kindest attentions, ... but, much more, they showed me themselves; who are so many of them very earnest, faithful, affectionate, some of them highly gifted men; *some of them, too, prepared to make great sacrifices for conscience's sake.* Froude is a noble youth to whom my heart warms; I shall soon see him again. Truly I became fond of these monks of Oxford."

Evidently there was one man in America to whom the devastating *Nemesis of Faith* did not come as a surprise.

Of course Thoreau learned of Froude from Emerson's lips, and read Emerson's copy of that "incendiary" book. That Thoreau should send Froude a copy of his own first book — then falling still-born from Munroe's press — was only natural, considering the downrightness of that chapter in the work fancifully termed "Sunday." Froude's letter to Thoreau is the acknowledgment of the gift, and what an acknowledgment: "I have a right to tell you that there is no man living upon this earth at present, whose friendship or whose notice I value more than yours."

These men had so much in common. Thoreau also had forsaken the faith of his fathers; but a serener 'pagan' never shattered the shrines of the Saints. He could say, as another of our latter-day renunciants has said, "I need no assurances, I am a man who is preoccupied of his own soul."

Thoreau was too solidly self-centred to need assurances; yet he had become an author, and, being flesh and blood, his heart went out to his book as doth a mother's to her first-born. But howsoever interpenetrated by a conviction, howsoever possessed by it, howsoever driven by it, even to the forsaking of all that makes life dear, howsoever swerveless and indomitable in service thereto, nevertheless the solitary Thinker becomes as an armed host so soon as his conviction is shared by another. "I have gone near to despair. I am growing not to despair, and I thank you for a helping hand." Such is the assurance that this long-hidden letter carried to Thoreau. His still-born book had found one fellow-man who *believed* it. One can readily imagine Thoreau reading that old letter in the leafy solitude of Walden woods, and the thought of his heart is written upon his sunburnt face: "My book may be a sealed volume to the multitude, 'caviare to the general,' but here is one to whom it is intelligible, speaking audibly to the soul of him. It is enough if the book were written for him alone: is not every true book written for only him who can understand its message?"

Froude had written, "I congratulate you on the age in which your work is cast." Never did any compliment go farther astray. Thoreau had been obliged to publish at his own risk, and he had gone deeply into debt for the edition of one thousand volumes. Little heed did the 'age' take of his 'cast.'

Four years after the date of Froude's assuring letter, Thoreau wrote in his journal: "For a year or two past my publisher, falsely so called, has been writing from time to time to ask what disposition should be made of the copies of *A Week on the Concord and Merrimack Rivers* still on hand, and at last suggesting that he had use for the room they occupied in his cellar. So I had them all sent to me here, and they have arrived to-day by express, filling the man's wagon, 706 copies out of an edition of 1000, which I bought of Munroe four years ago, and have been ever since paying for and have not quite paid for yet. The wares are sent to me at last, and I have an opportunity to examine my purchase. They are something more substantial than fame, as my back knows, which has borne them up two flights of stairs to a place similar to that to which they trace their origin. Of the remaining 290 and odd, 75 were given away, the rest sold. I now have a library of nearly 900 volumes, over 700 of which I wrote myself. Is it not well that the author should behold the fruits of his labor? My works are piled up on one side of my chamber as high as my head, my *opera omnia*. This is authorship, these are the works of my brain. There was just one piece of good luck in the venture. The unbound copies were tied up by the printer four years ago in stout paper wrappers, and inscribed:—

> H. D. Thoreau,
> Concord River,
> 50 cops.

so Munroe had only to cross out "River" and write "Mass.," and deliver them to the express-man at once. I can now see what I write for, the result of my labors. Nevertheless in spite of this result, sitting beside the inert mass of my works, I take up my pen to-night to record

Home of the Thoreau Family, Concord, Mass.

It was in his bedroom in the attic of this house that Thoreau piled the 706 unsold copies of his first book. He died in the front room on the ground floor to the right of the main entrance.

what thought or experience I may have had, with as much satisfaction as ever. Indeed I believe that the result is more inspiring and better for me than if a thousand had bought my wares. It affects my privacy less and leaves me freer."

From all that I can learn of Thoreau, I find no reason to doubt the sincerity of this imperturbability. I believed it to be sincere before I knew of the Froude letter; I am assured of it now that I have read it. Such are the secret sustainments of the Thinker, and such sustainments should be and ever will be vouchsafed; for is not he who brings a message to men an Ambassador from the Most High, and do not even the ravens feed such Ministers Plenipotentiary?

The assurance of the Fellow of Exeter College was grateful to the graduate of Harvard; but Belief is not the accident of a diploma or the prerogative of the aristocracy of Letters. Thoreau was to have another assurance, dearer no doubt to him because its source was so much nearer the soil.

II.

THE BROTHER AND SISTER.

IN one of the quietest of American villages there dwelt an earnest reader of the *Weekly Tribune* in the days when Horace Greeley was at his best. In one issue thereof he found George Ripley's review of Thoreau's second book, *Walden, or, Life in the Woods*. The reviewer had made many lengthy citations from this most awakening work, and the reading of these set aflame the heart of the distant reader. He wrote to the publishers for and obtained a copy. From the title-page of *Walden* he learned that Thoreau was also the author of another book, the still-born *Week on the Concord and Merrimack Rivers.* This particular work the Michigan man soon found that he could not get from the publishers of *Walden,* nor could they inform him where it might be had, so utterly had Munroe's publication disappeared from the market. But the tang of *Walden* had "touched the spot" and the hungry man was ravenous for a taste of the *Week.* He had to write to Thoreau himself asking where that book could be bought; and thus began the correspondence, which I shall read with whatever of explanation I may be able to give.

Please bear in mind the situation: piled up in that garret-chamber, 'as high as my head,' are the seven hundred rejected books—cast into the "age" and by it most unmistakably cast out. Four years had they lain in Munroe's cellar,—more than once had he tried to get rid of them, and at last had 'suggested' that while there appeared to be no earthly use for *them*, he, James Munroe, 'had use for the room they occupied in his cellar.' For two years and two months had they found friendly shelter in the garret of John Thoreau. Behold! an enthusiastic letter from a distant stranger; one man who will not rest until he has read the ignored *Week*. Observe, if you please, the quiet calm of Thoreau's reply.

Concord, Jan. 18*th*, 1856.
Dear Sir:

I am glad to hear that my " Walden" has interested you — that perchance it holds some truth still as far off as Michigan. I thank you for your note.

The " Week" had so poor a pub-

lisher that it is quite uncertain whether you will find it in any shop. I am not sure but authors must turn booksellers themselves. The price is $1.25. If you care enough for it to send me that sum by mail (stamps will do for change), I will forward you a copy by the same conveyance.

As for the "more" that is to come, I cannot speak definitely at present, but I trust that the mine — be it silver or lead — is not yet exhausted. At any rate, I shall be encouraged by the fact that you are interested in its yield.   Yours respectfully,

Henry D. Thoreau.

["So poor a publisher," indeed. It was this same James Munroe that published Emerson's *Nature;* and it took him twelve years to sell an edition of five hundred copies. Verily, "authors must turn booksellers themselves." "The price is $1.25." A copy of the first edition of Thoreau's *Week* for one dollar and twenty-five cents! Go to, thou author-bookseller, thou art not up to the trade values of books! Every one of the very volumes that James Munroe had no 'room' for, now finds warm welcome to the selectest of private libraries at —eighteen dollars a copy! If the reader wishes to recognize those copies which were bought from Thoreau himself he will turn to page 396. On the bottom margin he will find six lines written in pencil and by Thoreau himself: the addition being so much of the original text as was overlooked by the compositor.—ED.]

It is hardly fair that I should go any farther until I have told you some little about Thoreau's Michigan correspondent. He was born in 1817, the same year as Thoreau, and was once a student at Oberlin, Ohio. "They wanted to make a 'preacher' of me," said he — quickly adding in the manner of one who has just missed a peril, "Gracious! I had a narrow escape." In fact, my aged friend has all the qualifications for Thoreau's 'Sunday School.' Pity it is, but his 'doxy is not Orthodoxy because it is n't your 'doxy. His is the doubt that is born of the supremest humility. Few indeed are they that understand it; but it matters not. Whosoever has read *Walden* will readily understand what that book had in it for the "wandering sheep" that had escaped from the Oberlin fold; they will as readily imagine with what haste he forwarded the one dollar and a quarter for a copy of the *Week*.

Concord, Feb. 10, '56.
Dear Sir:

I forwarded to you by mail on the 31st of January a copy of my " Week," post paid, which I trust that you have received. I thank you heartily for the expression of your interest in " Walden" and hope that you will not be disappointed by the " Week." You ask how the former has been received. It has found an audience of excellent character, and quite numerous, some 2000 copies having been dispersed. I should consider it a greater success to interest one wise and earnest soul, than a million unwise and frivolous.

You may rely on it that you have the best of me in my books, and that

I am not worth seeing personally, the stuttering, blundering clod-hopper that I am. Even poetry, you know, is in one sense an infinite brag and exaggeration. Not that I do not stand on all that I have written—but what am I to the truth I feebly utter!

I like the name of your county—may it grow men as sturdy as its trees. Methinks I hear your flute echo amid the oaks. Is not yours, too, a good place to study theology? I hope that you will erelong recover your turtle-dove, and that it may bring you glad tidings out of that heaven in which it disappeared.

Yours sincerely,
Henry D. Thoreau.

["I am not sure but authors must turn booksellers themselves." Indeed!

"I should consider it a greater success to interest one wise and earnest soul than a million unwise and frivolous!" No wonder that James Munroe had not cellar-room for the books of such a "stuttering, blundering clod-hopper."—ED.]

After reading the *Week* the Michigan man wished to share the good tidings of great joy with others. There was a distant relation, an upright member of an orthodox sect; *he* must have a copy of the *Week:* it may show him how fast asleep he is! The book was mailed to the somnolent saint from Thoreau direct; but it had been as well to have sent a copy of *Eliot's Indian Bible.*

My aged friend chuckles when he tells you that this very copy of the *Week* was subsequently borrowed by a Presbyterian preacher and—never returned!

On the same occasion a copy of both *Walden* and the *Week* were ordered for a brother in California. These arrived safely; and they were read and pondered under the shade of the great Sequoias, in the silence of the forest primeval. Both author and reader are long since where no shadows cloud the page. In the *lumen siccum* of Eternity the Thinker has learned "what argument his life to his brother's creed had lent."

Concord, May 31st, '56.
Dear Sir:
  I forwarded by mail a copy of my " Week," post paid to . . . . , according to your order, about ten days ago, or on the receit [sic] *of your note.*
  I will obtain and forward a copy

of "*Walden*" and also of the "*Week*" to California, to your order, post paid, for $2.60. The postage will be between 60 and 70 cents.

I thank you heartily for your kind intentions respecting me. The West has many attractions for me, particularly the lake country and the Indians, yet I do foresee what my engagements may be in the fall. I have once or twice came near going West a-lecturing, and perhaps some winter may bring me into your neighborhood: in which case I should probably see you. Yet lecturing has commonly proved so foreign and irksome to me, that I think I could only use it to acquire the means with which to make an independent tour another time.

As for my pen, I can say that it is not altogether idle, though I have *finished nothing new in the book form. I am drawing a rather long bow, though it may be a feeble one, but I pray that the archer may receive new strength before the arrow is shot.*

With many thanks, yours truly,
Henry D. Thoreau.

When forwarding the money for the last books ordered, a likeness of Thoreau was solicited, and having learned in some way that Thoreau was "poor," a five-dollar bill was enclosed in payment for the books and the desired picture, and it was requested that Thoreau should keep the balance "for his trouble." The reply to this kindly device is characteristic.

Henry D. Thoreau, age 39.
From a daguerreotype by B. D. Maxham, of Worcester, Mass., taken in 1856.

Concord, Saturday, June 21st, '56.
Dear Sir:

On the 12 ult. I forwarded the two books to California, observing your directions in every particular, and I trust that Uncle Sam will discharge his duty faithfully. While in Worcester this week I obtained the accompanying daguerreotype—which my friends think is pretty good—though better looking than I.

Books and postage . .	$2.64
Daguerreotype . . .	.50
Postage	.16
	3.30

5 00
3 30   You will accordingly
find 1 70 enclosed with my shadow.

Yrs

Henry D. Thoreau.

Thoreau had a poor throat for charity soup, no matter how tastefully it had been flavored. "Books and postage, $2.64; Daguerreotype and its postage, .66; Total, $3.30. Balance due you $1.70, and you will accordingly find $1.70 enclosed with my shadow." This holograph presents the poorest chirography of them all, the signature differing markedly from all the others. Yes, there was a shadow on his face when he wrote, for this is the only letter signed, curtly enough, "Yrs." instead of the accustomed "Yours truly" or "sincerely."

A little matter, do you say? Precisely; but did it never occur to you that the significances of life are in just its "little matters"? It is what we do and how, when not the great world is the spectator, but when the self is alone with the selfhood; then the undertone of character is heard, the 'still small voice' speaking audibly to the soul above all the roaring din of the mighty Babylon of which so many of us are in such cowardly dread.

That now aged man with whom Thoreau was then corresponding is indeed a most remarkable man. But I question if he is at all adapted for the latitude and longitude of . . . . . [The editor takes the liberty of suppressing the name.] No; we are like the Baltimore oysters labelled "extra selects." We should only mortify in a can of common oysters; so we have an uncommon can of our own. The name, it is true, is n't 'blown in the bottle'; but it is stamped on our "tin." I do not believe we would allow such an one as Thoreau's correspondent in our select can; nor do I believe Thoreau would have written a line to an "extra select." However, this sterling man, who owes little to the school and less to the college, had vouchsafed unto him the divine gift of insight. He is one of that rare few who are endowed with prescient foresight; most of us have only a purblind hindsight. We see the landscapes of life only after they have been passed, we discern the great ones of life only after they are dead — we are the "extra selects"!

[The editor is utterly unable to account for this rude and wholly unwarrantable outburst. Not a city of its size contains more people that are 'nice to know'; not any the largest city outdoes it in culture and elegant refinement. The ex-professor was recently asked if he did not *mean* that we are the "extra elects." His reply is not adapted for polite ears. Though it may cost him the friendship of the ex-professor, the editor trusts that he, at least, has done his duty to Society.]

Thoreau's *meaning* in this universe is no more a secret to this untutored man dwelling in remote Michigan than it was to the learned Fellow of Exeter College or to that graduate of Harvard who pitched his tent in Concord and taught America to think. Can you imagine what it implies to have "discovered" Thoreau in those early days; or do you imagine that Nature's "extra selects" are marked with a stencil-plate? Try and imagine what a consuming fervor is enkindled when a true Book is speaking to the soul of a man—his heart with hero-worship all aflame. If you have been capable of doing this, then you can conceive what fervid letters were sent, in those earlier days, from one earnest man in the distant West to that imperturbable and self-possessed man in "old Concord," and that conception will invest the next of Thoreau's letters with something deeper than the mere surface-reading shows.

Concord, July 8th, '57.
Dear Sir:
You are right in supposing that I have not been Westward. I am very little of a traveller. I am gratified to hear of the interest you take in my books; it is additional encouragement to write more of them. Though

my pen is not idle, I have not published anything for a couple of years at least. I like a private life, and cannot bear to have the public in my mind.

You will excuse me for not responding more heartily to your notes, since I realize what an interval there always is between the actual and imagined author and feel that it would not be just for me to appropriate the sympathy and good will of my unseen readers.

Nevertheless, I should like to meet you, and if I ever come into your neighborhood shall endeavor to do so. Can't you tell the world of your life also? Then I shall know you, at least as well as you me.

   Yours truly,
    Henry D. Thoreau.

They never met in the flesh; but there is an old man in the West patiently waiting for a meeting where heart answers unto heart as face unto face in the refiner's silver.

An unbroken silence of more than two years followed this last letter. In the interval America was preparing to make history; chapters that should be written with her best blood and the first page with that of a hero— a man in whom was incarnated the high purpose of the Lord God Omnipotent.

There, in Virginia, Captain John Brown lay captive, "wounded and in prison." Even an Abolition paper called him a 'madman' for that which he had tried to do. The doughfaces of the North sweat clammily; the "friends of the Union" trembled for the safety of that fabric;

universal consternation petrified the people. In that supreme moment a single voice was lifted up in the vestry-room of the little church in Concord wherein the first American Congress had held solemn deliberations. It was a voice that spake under a protest in which joined alike Whig, Democrat, and Abolitionist. "That speech should not be uttered; it is unwise, injudicious; it will do more harm than good," etc., etc. "I did not send to you for advice, but to announce that I am to speak"—and speak he did. It was Sunday evening, the thirtieth of October. The very next evening that intrepid voice was heard again, in Tremont Temple, and yet again in Worcester on the Wednesday following. It was the voice of one man; one man in fifty millions having the courage of his convictions; one man God-appointed to show a nation its way as the darkness was gathering around it and not a politician had the courage to strike a match to light the flickering tallow-dip of Policy.

The Western man read accounts of this one fearless voice, and wrote to Thoreau asking for the words he alone had dared to speak.

Concord, Nov. 24th, '59.
Dear Sir:

The lectures which you refer to were reported in the newspapers, after a fashion. *The last one in some half dozen of them, and if I possessed one, or all, I would send them to you, bad as they are. The best, or at least longest one of the Boston Lecture was in the Boston "Atlas and Bee" of Nov. 2nd.—may be half the whole [speech]. There were others in the " Traveller," the " Journal," &c., of the same date.*

I am glad to know that you are interested to see my things, and I wish I had them in printed form to send to you. I exerted myself considerably to get the last discourse printed and sold for the benefit of Brown's family — but the publishers are afraid of pamphlets, and it is now too late.

I return the stamps which I have not used.

I shall be glad to see you if I ever come your way.

Yours truly,
Henry D. Thoreau.

This holograph is very striking in its mute significance. The words seemed to leap from Thoreau's pen.

In fifteen different instances two words are written without taking the pen from the paper, in eight others three are thus continuously written, and in one line there are four impetuously chained together. There is nothing of this in the other five holographs. But, curiously, the signature to this last is the largest, boldest, clearest, and by far the best of them all. It reminds one of John Hancock's sign-manual on the *Declaration of Independence*. Surely, Massachusetts writes a fine hand on occasion!

There remained for Thoreau only two years and a half of his *Lehrjahre:* then he was "translated." Translated? Do they not say that of a Bishop when he is exalted? Even so; but is not Thoreau also a "bishop of souls"? There is now no obscuring rafter between him and the Unspeakable One who clothed him in clay that he might do his appointed work in the Universe—this little world his seed-field. Yes, it is the right word; it is his sorrowing sister's word. He was "translated" one beautiful Spring morning. It was on the sixth of May, 1862.

And now that sister is the Concord correspondent of him who long had waited and hoped for Thoreau to "come this way."

Concord, June 24*th,* 1862.
Dear Sir:
It gives me pleasure to acknowledge your note of the 18*th instant, and I desire to thank you for the very friendly sympathy which you have manifested for us in this season of sorrow and affliction.*

My mother and myself are the only surviving members of a family once numbering six. My elder brother, for whom you enquire, died twenty years ago, next a precious sister was called, and three years since my dear Father left us.

My brother Henry's illness commenced a year ago last December. During seventeen months never a murmur escaped him. I wish that I could describe the wonderful simplicity and child-like trust with which he accepted every experience. As he said, "he never met with a disappointment in his life, because he always arranged so as to avoid it." "He learned when he was a very little boy that he must die, and of course he was not disappointed when his time came." Indeed we cannot feel that he has died, but rather [has] been translated.

On one occasion he remarked to me that he considered perfect disease as agreeable as perfect health, since the mind always conformed to the condition of the body.

I never knew any one who set so great a value on Time as did my brother; he continued to busy himself all through his sickness, and during the last few months of his life he edited many papers for the press, and he did not cease to call for his manuscripts till the last day of his life.

While we suffer an irreparable loss in the departure of my most

---

* "No man ever lived who paid more ardent and unselfish attention to his business."

John Weiss.

gifted brother, still we are comforted and cheered by the memory of his pure and virtuous soul; and it is a great consolation to know that he possessed a spirit so attuned to the beauties and harmonies of Nature that the color of the sky, the fragrance of the flowers and the music of the birds ministered unceasingly to his pleasure. He was the happiest of mortals. This world a paradise. "Where there is knowledge, where there is virtue, where there is beauty, where there is progress, there is now his home."

You ask the name of my brother's traveling companion. Mr. . . . , a near neighbor and intimate friend, most frequently accompanied him in his walks. In the lines on page twenty-second of "The Week" you

Henry D. Thoreau, age 37.
From a crayon portrait drawn in 1854 by Samuel W. Rowse.
The original is in the Concord Free Library.

will find a reference to this same friend. Mr. ... wrote the lines sung at my brother's funeral. So sincere is his friendship for Henry, that, I doubt not, any token of esteem you may bestow for his sake, upon him, will be acceptable.

Within a few weeks we have had some photographs taken from a crayon portrait of my brother. The crayon drawing was made two years before Henry sent you his Dauguerreotype. Will you accept the inclosed picture? His friends all consider it an excellent likeness. My mother unites with me in very kind regards to yourself. It would afford us pleasure to see you at any time. Concord is the home of many worthies, Emerson, Alcott, Hawthorne, Channing, &c., all valued friends of my brother.

I trust that you may be attracted to this neighborhood.

Yours very truly,
S. E. Thoreau.

P. S. I received, by to-day's mail, a very appreciative notice of my brother from the pen of Storrow Higginson, formerly a pupil in Mr. Sanborn's school. I think the article would interest you. It is contained in the May number of the "Harvard Magazine." In the "Atlantic Monthly" for August you may look for a memorial by Mr. Emerson.

"He considered perfect disease as agreeable as perfect health, since the mind always conformed to the condition of the body." Where is there a more memorable observation? One month before, Sophia had written to Mr. Ricketson: "You ask me for some particulars regarding Henry's illness. I feel like saying that Henry was never affected, never reached by it. I never saw such a manifestation of the power of spirit over matter. Very often I have heard him tell his visitors that he enjoyed existence as much as ever. He remarked to me that there was as much comfort in perfect disease as in perfect health, the mind always conforming to the condition of the body."

There is the difference of a single word in these two statements: "comfort" in one letter, "agreeable" in the other. If the sentiment had been "cooked" for dramatic effect, there would not have been the shadow of a variation.

Of all writers, Thoreau is he whom we must read believingly. Indeed, he had long before left evidence of the unimpeachable truthfulness of this remarkable death-bed declaration.

"I am confined to the house by bronchitis, and so seek to content myself with that quiet and serene life there is in a warm corner by the fireside, and see the sky through the chimney-top. Sickness should not be allowed to extend farther than the body. We need only retreat farther within us, to preserve uninterrupted the continuity of serene hours to the end of our lives. As soon as I find my chest is not of tempered steel and my heart of adamant, I bid goodby to them and look out for a new nature. I will be liable to no accidents."—*Journal, Feb'y* 14*th*, 1841.

Twenty-two years later, brought to the supreme test, he proved the genuineness of his philosophy. He takes his place beside Socrates, Epictetus, Marcus Aurelius:

"A soul supreme, in each hard instance tried."

The crayon portrait—now in the Concord Free Library—was drawn by Samuel Worcester Rowse, and may safely be accepted as 'an excellent likeness' of Thoreau without a beard. Writing from England to Professor Norton, the poet Clough bears this testimony to the fidelity of Rowse's crayons: "Child brought me your present of Emerson's picture, which is really, I think, the best portrait of any living and known-to-me man that I have ever seen. It is a great pleasure to possess it." One year later, he had not changed his mind:—"When is Rowse coming over? Will you give him a letter to me? I continue to think his picture of Emerson the best portrait I know of anyone I know."

Sophia Thoreau's letter was written seven weeks after her brother's death,—the fresh wound still bleeding. Poor, stricken, lonely sister! Bereaved of such a brother, mourning for the 'irreparable loss,' yet prouder of her brother dead than of the countless carcases strutting in the sunlight and kept from stinking only by the cheap salt of civilization. Poor Sophia! she was quoting from her recollections of that beautiful spring day when Emerson spoke the eulogy over her brother's coffin. But, pardonably enough, she had misquoted. Emerson had said: "His soul was made for the noblest society; he had in a short time exhausted the capabilities of this world; wherever there is knowledge, wherever there is virtue, wherever there is beauty, he will find a home." He also said: "The scale on which his studies proceeded was so large as to require longevity, and we were the less prepared for his sudden disappearance. The country knows not yet, or in the least part, how great a son it has lost. It seems an injury that he should leave in the midst of his broken task, which none else can finish,— a kind of indignity to so noble a soul that it should depart out of Nature before yet he has been shown to his peers for what he is. But he, at least, is content."

O my friends, having the clear testimony of his sister's letter and also Emerson's confirmation of Thoreau's deep 'content,' can we not say with that sister, "of course he was not disappointed when his time came." But, can such a life be in any sense a failure, in any sense be incomplete; is an early home-call an 'injury'; is it indeed an 'indignity' to be summoned from this pitiful Vanity Fair by the Master of the Vineyard?

Concord, Oct. 20, 1862.
Dear Friend:

Absence from home together with illness must be my apology for not before acknowledging your last kind letter.

Certainly it will give me much pleasure to present the walking-cane which you propose to send to Mr. . . . . . , who feels keenly the depar-

ture of my precious brother, and who will value any token of friendship shown to his memory.

I am very glad that you have seen Higginson's article. It was an outburst of affection from his young heart which gratified me much.

I was fortunate lately in receiving from Mr. Emerson a specimen of the "*Edelweisse*," Gnaphalium leontopodium, which was sent to him by a friend who brought the plant from Tyrol. How I wish dear Henry could have seen it.

I can never tell you how much I enjoyed copying and reading aloud my brother's manuscripts last winter when he was preparing them for the press. The paragraph which you quote from the essay on "Walking" impressed and charmed me particularly, I remember; and I am glad to hear you express your satisfaction in regard to the whole article.

I doubt not that ere this you have enjoyed the paper on "Autumnal Tints." I am sure that my dear Brother went to his grave as gracefully as the leaves in autumn. [The poor sister means, as undisturbedly as the leaf flashes into all the gleaming glory of the rainbow and silently obeys the Divine behest that ordains its death when Autumn winds grow chill.] Oh! that you could have known him personally: he was wonderfully gifted in conversation. [Aye; and now there is only silence and the patient waiting for the gracious manumission of Death!]

Thank you for the hints relating to yourself and family. What you say about enjoying the days as if they were made expressly for your-

self denotes a spirit of rare contentment, which I am happy to know you possess.

My mother joins with me in kind regards to yourself and family.

Trusting to see you at some future time, I remain,

        Very truly yours,
            S. E. Thoreau.

There has been no abatement in that 'spirit of rare contentment.' That quiet home in the West is radiant therewith, as I can testify. Cheerful and serene, the old-time friend of Thoreau and "Mother" are meekly waiting,—

"Their faces shining with the light
  Of duties beautifully done."

Concord, March 4th, 1863.
Dear Friend:

I am happy to inform you of the safe arrival of the cane. The package reached me last evening.

It was with mingled feelings of pleasure and pain that I looked on this gift—a rare instance of friendship, most worthily bestowed.

I handed the cane at once to Mr. . . . . . , who expressed great satisfaction.

The article is very chaste and beautiful. I should like to know the name of the wood.

Allow me to thank you for this token; it would have been fully appreciated by my departed brother.

Mr. . . . . . will communicate with you. [Which he certainly did and after the manner of his species.]

It may interest you to know that our afflictions have been heightened by an accident which happened to my dear mother, early in the season: —she fell down a long staircase, breaking her right arm and otherwise seriously injuring herself. Now, however, she is slowly recovering, and joins with me in very kind remembrances to yourself and family.
Yours truly,
S. E. Thoreau.

"Allow *me* to thank you." The italics are in the original. "Mr. . . . will communicate with you"—though in what manner this deponent saith not. This is the meaning of the italicised "me." Well, here is the 'communication' from the recipient of a most unique cane, originally designed for Thoreau himself, but arriving from distant California too late.

Concord, March 4, 1863.
Dear Sir:
The cane arrived at this place last evening and was delivered to me, in perfect order.
X. Y. Z.

I have in my keeping the very express-receipt that was issued to the donor of the cane, and it contains just as much pathos as the recipient's "communication"—and not an iota less! This cold-storage 'communication' of Mr. X. Y. Z. is *sui generis*—and yet we are told that only the amphibia have oval blood-corpuscles.

The cane was of manzanita wood, the handle was made from a buffalo horn, and the silver mountings were engraved with appropriate quotations from Thoreau's writings. It was a pious thank-offering from the two brothers — one in the far West and the other in California; but Death was swifter than friendship, and the belated tribute was given to the dead man's dearest friend. X. Y. Z.'s notelet contains just sixteen words, not one of which will spell "Thanks"; but there are two and one-half pages of "Complementary mottoes," nineteen in all: as if this grateful friend of Thoreau had said, "Two can play at that game!" Verily, we are "fearfully and wonderfully made."

I hold in my hand Sophia Thoreau's last letter to the Western man. Her mother had died, the broken home had become to the solitary mourner as a grave; its every room was haunted by the "old familiar faces," but the dear lips are silent—and that is the silence that kills.

Concord, May 24th, 1873.
Dear Mr. . . . . . :

After several weeks' absence, I returned yesterday to Concord, to find the volume of poems you had so kindly forwarded, and without stopping to cut the leaves I hasten to thank you most heartily for this friendly remembrance.

Just now I am about to leave Concord, and shall make my home in Bangor, Maine. Mr. F. B. Sanborn's family will occupy my house.

Perhaps you are aware that my precious mother departed a year since.

You will be interested to know that Mr. Channing has written a memoir of my brother, which will soon appear.

Mr. X. Y. Z. is as whimsical as ever — not calling at my house or recognizing me on the street for the past six years.

We are looking for Mr. Emerson's return [from Europe] *and the town will give him a cordial reception. I hope you may see our village again: its charms increase from year to year.*

I promise myself much pleasure in the poems when a little leisure is afforded me.

Please excuse this hasty note and believe me,

Yours truly,
S. E. Thoreau.

Twelve days after the burial of her brother Henry, Sophia Thoreau wrote to Mr. Daniel Ricketson: "Profound joy mingles with my grief. I feel as if something beautiful had happened —not death."

And something beautiful had indeed happened—another of the countless miracles that surround us here: a soul leveling this lift that it may go on to a higher; a soul that also had for its last countersign the "Æquanimitas" of the dying Roman Emperor; a soul that found 'perfect disease as agreeable as perfect health'; a soul to which this world was a paradise—a "Paradise Regained" by the clear sanity of supreme submission to the Maker; a soul that at the home-call left the only paradise it had ever seen and the purest delights that mere man can ever know,—left all as serenely and grandly as the setting sun sinks through the purple glory whose last refulgence gives the promise of another day.

Sophia Thoreau bade farewell to the "charming village" wherein she had known the unspeakable delight of companionship with such a brother and also the unutterable pang of parting which that 'something beautiful' we call 'death' entails. Think of her loneliness, of her last visit to that quiet hilltop in *Sleepy Hollow:* father, mother, sister, and brothers *there;* she the last lone lingerer here.

She was in Bangor two short years, and then "something beautiful" happened again: a family reunion where the amaranth forever blooms, where there is no night, where never a tear is known save those of that Divine compassion which is "touched with the feeling of our infirmities."

Sophia E. Thoreau.
From a daguerreotype found among her effects
after her death. Heretofore unpublished.

APPENDIX.

Two Visits to Concord, Mass.
From an old Diary.

Sept. 1st, 1863. Arrived at Concord about 5 p. m. Stopped at the Middlesex House. Soon after, went across the way to a bookstore and bought a copy of the "Boston Commonwealth." On the first page found Thoreau's poem "The Departure,"

In this roadstead I have ridden.

This is the first publication of it. I accepted it as a sort of introduction meant for *me*.

This [place] appears like a quite orderly, staid New England town and somewhat reminds me of Oberlin, Ohio, twenty years ago.

Somehow, I feel a singular contentedness and as if my good genius had, for the time, got the upper hand of all obstacles and alone presided. In the morning, if my health will permit, intend viewing some scenes and places more dear to me than I can well tell.

Sept. 2nd. After breakfast went into the "old" and also the "new" burying ground; then to the new cemetery—"Sleepy Hollow." The ground is rolling and finely shaded with pines and oaks. Did not find what I was in pursuit of. Enquired of a man at work there where the Thoreaus' burying place was. He said, "At the new grounds." I also asked if I pronounced the name *Thoreau* right. Went to the place specified and found one grave with headstone marked, "John Thoreau, Jr.," and another near by newer and unmarked.

Then left for the Walden woods by the old Lincoln road. Found the pond, beanfield and site of Thoreau's house. The beanfield is now growing trees, pine, birch, etc., in rows, quincunx order—a fine sight!

P. M. To the old Battle-ground back of the old Manse. Found two other men there, visitors like myself. One of them read off the inscriptions on the monument in a clear, loud tone of voice, bordering somewhat on the pompous.

After supper at the hotel, called upon the Thoreaus, mother and sister. Found them rather expecting me. Was made quite welcome and urgently requested to get my things from the hotel and stop with them—did so.

They are decidedly bright-appearing women

—the mother, I should say, about sixty-five, the daughter [Sophia] forty. The conversation drifted readily to [the subject of] the son and brother. Mr. X. called and planned a walk for both of us to-morrow. Found him sociable and attentive. During the evening more talk about Thoreau's last illness. His mother said: "Why, this room [their parlor] did not seem like a sick-room. My son wanted flowers and pictures and books all around here; and he was always so cheerful and wished others to be so while about him. And during the nights he wanted the lamp set on the floor and some chairs put around it so that in his sleepless hours he could amuse himself with watching the shadows."

Sept. 4. Fitful sleeping last night: too full of thinking. This A. M. called upon Alcott with Miss Thoreau. Had a fine interview with him. He talked about Carlyle, Thoreau, books, his own experience, etc. I did not see his daughter Louise. She had just come back from the Army Hospital at Washington; had lost part of her hair and so was unpresentable.

This P. M., X. Y. Z. and I took our walk. Went off to the S. W. of the village (on 'the old Marlborough Road,' I think) and finally struck Concord river in a curve where X. said he and Thoreau used to go in bathing. X. wanted me to repeat that performance with him; I let him go in, while I took notes. The opposite and sunward bank is lined with a thick growth of evergreens which cast their dark shadow into the water below. The faint ripple on its surface gave the view the appearance of an inverted forest seen through a huge sheet of frosted glass. From here we went up on to the Concord Cliffs. X. showed me the Hollowell Place, Baker Farm, and the house where John Field the Irishman once lived. Thence to Walden Pond through a growth of young timber, where X. showed me a patch, a rod or so square, of "American Yew" [*Taxus Canadensis*] which, he said, Thoreau was very partial to, not showing it to everybody.

From the Pond and house-plot (the building itself has been moved away some three miles North) through the deserted beanfield, to the Lincoln Road where, following North, through a hollow, X. pointed out to me, a few rods away, "Brister's Spring," whither I went, lay down and took a good, cold drink to the memory of the writer who has given it its consequence.

Sept. 4th. At home with the Thoreau family. P. M. Went with Miss Thoreau up, N. W., on to the hill ("Nashawtuck"?). A fine view! Ponkawtasset off to the N. E. a mile or so.

The Assabet, at the north of us, winding its way to the Concord River below. The old North Bridge, the Monument near by and the village spread out in its beauty.

Sept. 5th. A. M. Took a ride with the two Misses Thoreau, maiden aunts of Thoreau, and Sophia. Called on Mr. [Edmund] Hosmer — not at home. Then on Mr. Platt; a pleasant time with him. Afterwards drove to Mr. Bull's home. He is the originator of the Concord grape that I had already sent for. Found Mr. B. a splendid talker and an enthusiastic garden man. P. M. Went alone to Walden Pond. Took a swim in it. Called at the patch of *American Yew* and at the Cliffs. Evening with the Thoreaus at their home.

Sept. 6th. Before breakfast, visited the "new" burying ground. Found Thoreau's grave. After breakfast, took quite a walk, N. E. of the town and mostly in the woods. (I have doubtless crossed and recrossed the dear, absent man's path so many times in this morning's trip!) Found, on my return, that Mr. Hosmer had been at the Thoreaus' to return my call of yesterday. Went soon after dinner to see him and stayed there until X. came, by agreement, to visit the "Estabrook Country" (they call it) to take a look at the Thoreau hut. It had been moved there some years before. Took a memento, a broken shingle, as a fitting emblem. Here is the field of boulders, some from eight to ten feet high, and such clumps of barberry bushes! Evening at Mrs. Horace Mann's with Miss Thoreau. Met there Miss Elizabeth Peabody, Mrs. Mann's sister, and her eldest son [Mrs. Horace Mann's], who accompanied Thoreau on his trip West seeking health. Found the young man greatly interested in Botany. Miss Peabody spoke very feelingly and freely of Margaret Fuller of blessed memory.

Sept. 7th. Arose rather early this morning and took a walk westward some mile and a half to a mill on the Assabet. On returning, found a branch from a young maple already turned of a fire-red, a part of which I broke off and took back with me and threw up into the branches of an evergreen that faced one side of the Thoreau house. After breakfast, it caught Mrs. Thoreau's eye and she began wondering what it meant. When I showed her, she exclaimed: "There! that was just like my son, Henry." I could n't help but feel a little flattered.

Afternoon. Took a ride up the Assabet with Mr. S. That was a very pleasant interview: Mr. S. seemed so easily to make it such — he talked so kindly and well of Thoreau.

After this, called upon Mr. Alcott, in company with X., also upon Mr. Emerson. A pleasant fifteen or twenty minutes' interview. Mr. Emerson enquired if I knew much about the Michigan University; spoke in high terms of President Tappan; asked if the young men of the West were not, some of them at least, seeking for more light and truth.

After dinner, when I bade the Thoreaus good bye, Mrs. Thoreau's sister, having come down from her room, stood at the foot of the stairs weeping. It was a tender leave-taking.

Second Visit to Concord.

Eleven years later.

August 27th, 1874. At the Middlesex House once more, arriving a little after noon. Dined and then started for Walden Pond. On my way out, on the Lincoln Road, I stopped at Brister's Spring, and as it had become a sacred fountain, I lay down and deliberately drank seven swallows of its cool, clear water to the memory of its absent poet. And now upon the site of that house in which Henry

Thoreau lived nearly thirty years ago, I sit writing up this diary of to-day.

It is a beautiful place! The book "Walden," telling of his life here, first notified me of its author and his writings: that formed an epoch in my life.

The cabin is gone, long since moved away, but, Thank God! they cannot move this foundation nor the pleasant memories.

Passed along the pond side toward the S. W. to find the Concord Cliffs. Found a man in charge of the picnic grounds on the railroad side of the pond, of whom I enquired the way. He had never heard of such a place, but I got there all the same. The vale, lake, river running through it, looked much as they did eleven years ago. The [Irishman's] house on the Baker Farm has disappeared. Went around West and North to the village, and then to *Sleepy Hollow* cemetery. I found all the Thoreau graves (the remains having been removed thither since my visit, eleven years ago) up back on a little, shaded hill, and having neat, plain brown headstones. A little farther on I found a short, thick slab of marble, at the head of a grave and on it was marked "Hawthorne." A silent farewell to the graves of the Thoreaus and then I went to the hotel.

After supper went to visit once more the old

Burial-plot of the Thoreau Family.
The grave of Henry's brother John is behind the large stone, between Sophia and Helen.

Battle-ground and the Monument. On my return, took a look at the new monument (erected to the memory of the fallen friends in the late war) standing on the public square. When here before in '63, it was war time and soldiers were being mustered into service, and they were encamped on the same open square. *Now* only some of their *names* are on record *there*. Such is life!

Aug. 29*th*. Arose at 5 o'clock and took an early walk on North side of R. R. This *is* a grand old town! How quiet and restful the people seem! After breakfast went to call upon X. His housekeeper went up stairs and notified him, and he came down with quite a visible scowl on his countenance, but when I told him who I was, he soon called me to mind, brightened up, was quite cordial and made me welcome to his room below, for reading, writing, and so forth. I accepted this offer with pleasure, in the meantime making an arrangement for a walk together in the afternoon.

2 o'clock, P. M. Started out with Mr. X. for a trip of over one and a half or two miles S. E., on what they call the Old Virginia Road, to see the house where Thoreau was born. I found my companion a little captious and uneasy — I did not keep to the foot-path

beside the road! In our conversing, I forgot to do it, which seemed to annoy him. (His whims showed themselves otherwise during that walk.)

We found the house; X. was good-natured and communicative; he pointed out to me the corner room wherein Channing's "Poet-Naturalist" first saw daylight. We returned by the way of Mr. Alcott's, took tea with the family and stayed there until nearly nine o'clock. The older daughter, Louise, was away from home, but I met her sister May. She is quite an artist; bright, active, a good talker, somewhat forward, and she reminded me of some shrewd, sprightly young man that had travelled. She is quite busy, painting and selling her work — her father said — to raise money for taking a third trip to Europe. For a few moments I thought of patronising her a little; so, pricing a piece of her painting on a black panel about the size of a chair slat, I found it to be $25.00. I "threw up the sponge."

Mr. A. read to me from the manuscript of a forthcoming book. I liked it much, but X. became visibly restive (A. noticed it) and finally left the room to go and talk with the women. Afterwards, X. evidently felt that he had misdone, so on leaving he protested that he was interested in hearing A.'s writings read by him, and he made an appointment thereupon to go with me there tomorrow afternoon for that very purpose. Returned to the hotel at 9.30 P. M. (*The idea of repeating that call at Alcott's to gratify a whim!*)

Aug. 30th. Up at six o'clock for a walk past the old Monument and up Ponkawtasset hill, on the side of which William Ellery Channing once lived and got the credit for going farther to visit Thoreau in his hut in midwinter than any other living man — "*that was not a poet!*" It was pleasant to stand there and see the placid Concord running through the meadows, where thirty-five years ago, near this time of the year, Henry Thoreau and his brother rowed down this stream upon that trip on the account whereof were strung the beads that glitter and gleam in Thoreau's first book.

In the afternoon, called upon X. to go to Mr. Alcott's *to hear him read.* A. did "read"; and X. and I sat and [X.] very civilly listened to him.

During the reading Mrs. Alcott came in, and I had the pleasure of making farther acquaintance with her. She seemed a kind, sweet, motherly woman. After the reading broke up, a pleasant general chat ensued.*

---

* "A general chat" — and Alcott, the Great Converser, present! We trust that our diarist is truthful. — ED.

Tea was announced, and contrary to my intention, I ate there again. After that Alcott gave me some of his books.

Mr. S. had learned that I was in town. So he found X. and myself and invited us to his house this evening. I found that he was living in the Thoreau home of eleven years ago. In the meantime Mrs. Thoreau has died, and her daughter, Sophia, gone to live with relatives in Maine. He gave me some interesting information about William B. Wright, author of "The Brook and other Poems," Shelley's later publishers, Walt Whitman, John Burroughs, Wilson Flagg, etc. After which cake and ale were served, and X. and I left.

Aug. 31st. Arose this morning about Four o'clock and started for a last visit to Walden Pond. I shall probably not see it again. Here I sit with my back against a little pine sapling, now growing on the site where once stood the hut. A few feet in front of me is a small but gradually increasing pile of stones to which every friend of Thoreau is expected to add his unit. I brought one up from the pond as my contribution and pencilled on it the word "Bethel." I also set out near by a plant of "Life-everlasting" that I had found while on the way here.

As I sit here facing the pond, I observe on

my left, about fourteen or fifteen rods distant, a grove of those tall "arrowy" pines, such as Thoreau used for his house-building twenty-nine years ago. There is apparently not a breath of air stirring. Birds are singing about me and even the hum of an occasional mosquito is still heard. I left the pond, passing out by the beanfield. The grove of trees that Thoreau planted thereon in payment for his occupancy, looked quite sorry from the effects of a fire that had run through there some time previously.

A very genial last visit to X. He gave me a number of books, just as he had done at my first visit. As I bade him good bye, saying this would be my last visit to Concord—that I should not see it again, he answered: "Oh, yes, you will."

Our last glimpse of Thoreau's Western correspondent shall be a fragment from one of his letters to Thoreau's sister, Sophia.

"I often meet your brother in my dreams and with this peculiarity about these meetings: while, as you know, our night-visions are often abnormal, grotesque, and disappointing, in this case I uniformly find my high ideal of him while [I am] awake, fully sustained. Occasionally he has become as it were transfigured to me, beyond my power to describe. So I have for some time been in the habit of associating him with the North polestar, as through every hour of the twenty-four it keeps its one position in the heavens."

It is much to have inspired such a friendship, and it passeth riches to have been capable of such an inspiration. It fitly marks an epoch in a man's life.

www.ingramcontent.com/pod-product-compliance
Lightning Source LLC
Chambersburg PA
CBHW031337160426
43196CB00007B/709